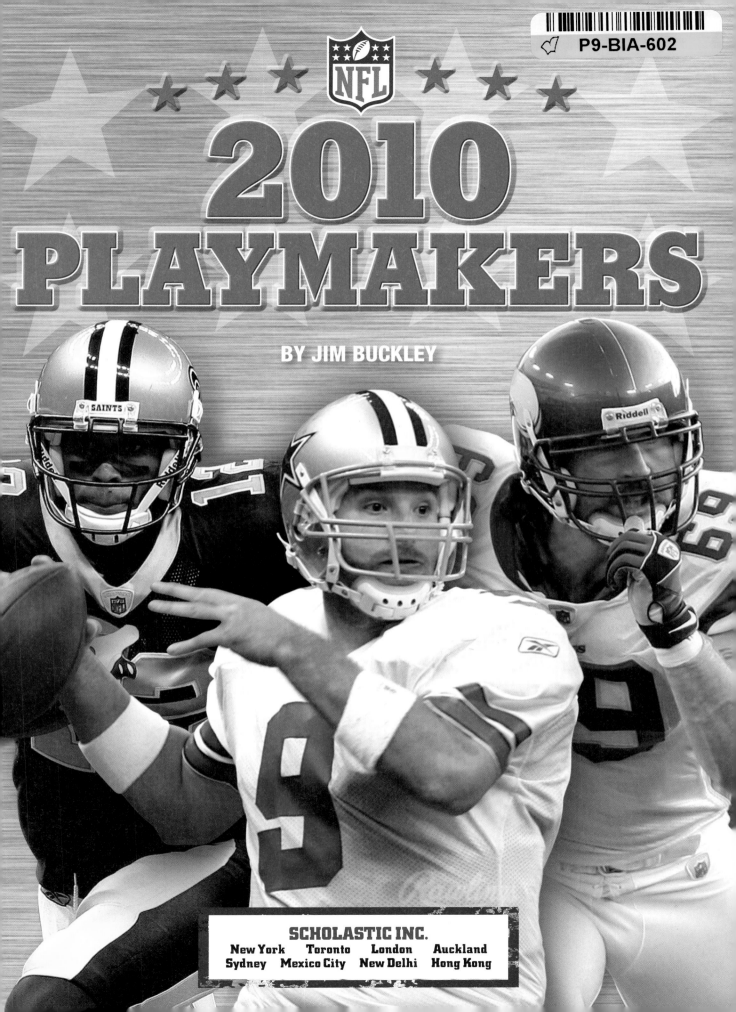

P9-BIA-602

NFL

2010 PLAYMAKERS

BY JIM BUCKLEY

SCHOLASTIC INC.
New York   Toronto   London   Auckland
Sydney   Mexico City   New Delhi   Hong Kong

Front cover: (l to r) © Chris Graythen/Getty Images; © Scott Halleran/Getty Images; © Scott Boehm/Getty Images

Back cover: (left) © Al Pereira/Getty Images; (center & right) © Al Messerschmidt/Getty Images

Interior:

p. 4: © Ronald Martinez/Getty Images; p. 5: © Scott Halleran/Getty Images;

p. 6: © Kevin Terrell/AP Images; p. 7: © Harry How/Getty Images; p. 8: © Ronald Martinez/Getty Images;

p. 9: © Al Messerschmidt/Getty Images; p. 10: © Jonathan Ferrey/Getty Images; p. 11: © Andy Lyons/Getty Images;

p. 12: © Paul Spinelli/AP Images; p. 13: © Jim McIsaac/Getty Images; p. 14: © Al Messerschmidt/Getty Images;

p. 15: © Al Messerschmidt/Getty Images; p. 16: © Scott Boehm/Getty Images; p. 17: © Al Messerschmidt/Getty Images;

p. 18: © Andrew Hancock/Sports Illustrated/Getty Images; p. 19: © Kevin C. Cox/Getty Images; p. 20: © Getty Images;

p. 21: © Al Messerschmidt/Getty Images; p. 22: © George Gojkovich/Getty Images; p. 23 © Scott Boehm/Getty Images;

p. 24: © Paul Jasienski/Getty Images; p. 25: © Paul Spinelli/AP Images; p. 26: © Scott Boehm/Getty Images;

p. 27: © Wesley Hitt/Getty Images; p. 28: © Michael Zagaris/Getty Images; p. 29: © Ezra Shaw/Getty Images;

p. 30: © Bill Kostroun/AP Images; p. 31: © Al Pereira/Getty Images; p. 32: © Bill Nichols/AP Images

No part of this work may be reproduced, stored in a retrieval system, or transmitted in any form or by any means, electronic, mechanical, photocopying, recording, or otherwise without written permission of the publisher. For information regarding permission, write to Scholastic Inc, Attention: Permissions Department, 557 Broadway, New York, NY 10012.

ISBN 978-0-545-21853-5

The NFL and individual NFL member team identifications, photographs, and other content used on or in this publication are trademarks, copyrighted designs, and other forms of intellectual property of NFL, Inc., and the respective NFL member teams and may not be used, in whole or part, without the prior written consent of NFL, Inc. All rights reserved.

Copyright © 2010 by NFL, Inc.

All rights reserved. Published by Scholastic Inc. SCHOLASTIC and associated logos are trademarks and/or registered trademarks of Scholastic Inc.

12 11 10 9 8 7 6 5 4 3 2 1   10 11 12 13 14 15/0

Printed in the U.S.A.   40
First printing, July 2010

INTRODUCTION

An exciting National Football League game comes complete with amazing passing, line-busting running, acrobatic catches, and clutch tackles. And so does this book! Thanks to the amazing athletes you'll meet in these pages, an NFL game is packed with play after play of excitement. These players are the best of the best, the guys whose talent, drive, and effort helped them climb the ladder of football success.

Some of them arrived after award-winning college careers. Others blossomed once they reached the pros. Still others waited for the chance to shine—and then grabbed it. But they all share one trait: the drive to succeed. They don't let anything get in their way, whether that means opposing tacklers and blockers, or the hours of training needed to be an NFL player.

As you read on—and as you follow the NFL on TV and via *NFL.com*—you will be thrilled by these players' stunning skills. But if you want to join them someday, remember that they put in years of work to reach their current spots.

So get started now . . . and maybe someday we'll be writing about you!

TONY ROMO

QB, DALLAS COWBOYS
6-2, 226
EASTERN ILLINOIS UNIVERSITY

Tony Romo's NFL career reads like a movie. When he wasn't drafted after a great college career, Romo was signed as a free agent by the Cowboys in 2003. He worked hard as a backup until a game against the Giants in 2006. Then, at halftime, the Dallas coaches made a switch: You're the man, Tony. Go get 'em.

Romo took over as the leader of one of the NFL's most storied teams. A dream come true, right?

Not quite. It took a little longer for Romo to rise to the top. Romo helped Dallas reach the wild-card playoff game after the 2006 season. In fact, he almost led them to victory. But as the Cowboys tried to attempt a short field goal to win the game, Romo dropped the snap . . . and the Cowboys' season was over.

CAREER STATS				
Years	Comp.	Att.	Yards	TDs
7	1,178	1,857	15,045	107

Did he quit? Did he let his mistake ruin his years of work? No, said Romo. He returned in 2007 to throw a career-high 36 touchdowns and make the Pro Bowl. He's been a top NFL passer ever since.

In 2009, Romo brought the Cowboys back to the playoffs. And this time, there was no dropping of the snap. By leading Dallas to a 34–14 win over Philadelphia, Romo guided Dallas to its first playoff victory since 1996.

This popular, strong-armed QB has lots more left in his career, but he's shown that he's already putting on a heck of a show.

TONY ROMO

PEYTON MANNING

QB, INDIANAPOLIS COLTS
6-5, 230
UNIVERSITY OF TENNESSEE

Sammy Baugh. Otto Graham. Johnny Unitas. Joe Montana. Those are the names that many longtime NFL fans put at the top of the "all-time quarterbacks" list. Peyton Manning has shown that he deserves to be among them. In 2009, Manning became the first player ever to win four NFL Most Valuable Player awards. In a year in which his Colts didn't have a strong running game and in the first season without his long-time target Marvin Harrison on board, Manning led the Colts to 14 regular-season wins.

He capped his fourth MVP campaign off with a spot in Super Bowl XLIV, the second of his amazing career.

That game wrapped up a phenomenal decade for the QB. He led the Colts to an NFL-record 115 wins in the 2000s, more than any other team in any other decade. The Colts won the AFC South five times and also won Super Bowl XLI. And Manning was one of only two quarterbacks named to the NFL's All-Decade Team of the 2000s.

His records would fill this whole book, but here are a few big ones:

—10 seasons with 4,000 or more passing yards (with a career high of 4,557 in 2004)

—49 TD passes in 2004, an all-time record until topped by Tom Brady's 50 in 2007

—192 straight games started from the beginning of a career

—Colts records for attempts, completions, touchdown passes, and passing yards

Manning has become the NFL's most well-known player, appearing in funny TV commercials and on TV comedy shows. Of course, he's also part of the NFL's most famous quarterback family. His dad, Archie, was a star for the New Orleans Saints in the 1970s. His brother Eli led the New York Giants to victory in Super Bowl XLII, a year after Peyton earned his own Super Bowl MVP trophy.

When you're talking about football with your kids someday, you'll be able to say that you watched one of the best quarterbacks—if not the best quarterback—of all time . . . in his prime!

CAREER STATS

Years	Comp.	Att.	Yards	TDs
12	4,232	6,531	50,128	366

PEYTON MANNING

MATT SCHAUB

QB, HOUSTON TEXANS
6-5, 240
UNIVERSITY OF VIRGINIA

Quick—who led the NFL in passing yards in 2009? Peyton Manning? Drew Brees? Aaron Rodgers? No, no, and no. The king of the air was Matt Schaub of the Houston Texans with 4,770 yards. In his third full season running the Houston offense, Schaub continued his climb to a spot among the NFL's elite QBs.

Along with his league-leading yardage, Schaub earned a permanent place in Houston Texans' history. By leading his team to a Week 17 victory over the Patriots, Schaub assured Houston of the first winning record in its history.

Schaub joined Houston in 2007 after three seasons with Atlanta. While acting as a backup with the Falcons, he showed enough flashes of talent that the Texans traded to make him their number-one QB.

CAREER STATS

Years	Comp.	Att.	Yards	TDs
6	923	1,413	11,087	59

Injuries slowed him a bit in 2007 and 2008, but in 2009, he started all 16 games. Teaming with star receiver Andre Johnson, Schaub quickly showed Houston fans why the team had made that big trade. In the final game of the season against a powerful New England, Schaub led the Texans to three straight touchdowns in the fourth quarter. That rally to victory—they finished the season with four straight wins—gave the team a 9–7 record. Schaub's skills and his team's late-season success mean good things are ahead for this young QB and his squad.

MATT SCHAUB

CHRIS JOHNSON

RB, TENNESSEE TITANS
5-11, 200
EAST CAROLINA UNIVERSITY

About the only thing faster than the career start Chris Johnson has had is Chris Johnson himself! The Titans' running back electrified the NFL in 2009 by becoming the sixth player ever to top 2,000 yards in a season. Johnson's 2,006 yards were the most since Baltimore's Jamal Lewis had 2,066 yards in 2003.

Johnson's greatest weapon is his speed. He can bust past a linebacker with the best of them, but it's his breakaway wheels that provided many of his amazing runs. In fact, he scored three touchdowns on runs of 85 yards or more in

CAREER STATS

Years	Att.	Yards	TDs	Rec.	Rec. Yds.	Rec. TDs
2	609	3,234	23	93	763	3

2009. No other running back has ever done that . . . in a *career*!

Among his 16 total TDs in 2009, Johnson also had two other runs over 50 yards and a pair of TD receptions that covered more than half the field. Wow!

Also, by adding 503 receiving yards, Johnson set an NFL single-season record with 2,509 yards from scrimmage. That topped Marshall Faulk's 1999 mark of 2,429 yards.

Johnson had a terrific rookie season in 2008, with 1,488 rushing yards and nine rushing touchdowns. But he really busted out in 2009, announcing his presence with a 91-yard TD run, a 57-yard TD run, and a 69-yard TD catch in Week 2 against Houston.

Every defender in the NFL will be watching Johnson in 2010 . . . but they'll probably be watching him run away down the field for a touchdown!

CHRIS JOHNSON

JOSH CRIBBS

WR/KR, CLEVELAND BROWNS
6-1, 215
KENT STATE UNIVERSITY

The Cleveland Browns offense loves watching Josh Cribbs return kickoffs. With his record-breaking skills, kicking off to the Browns often means that the team's offense is about to get a break! Since joining the Browns in 2005, Cribbs has become the best all-time at returning kickoffs for scores. With a pair of thrilling runs in a December 2009 game against Kansas City, Cribbs set a new NFL career mark with eight kickoff-return touchdowns—and he's only 26!

He's not just a return specialist, either. Cribbs has done it all: running the ball, catching passes, returning punts, and even throwing passes. In 2009, he really was in a groove. Cribbs led the NFL with three kickoff-return TDs and added a TD on a punt return. He also had a touchdown catch and a scoring run! His size, versatility, speed, and energy have made him a true football "Mr. Everything."

CAREER STATS

Years	KO Ret.	Yds.	TDs
5	265	7,049	8

On offense, Cribbs' skills have emerged as the Browns, like many teams, added a "wildcat" formation. These plays try to get the ball into the hands of a team's most elusive player. It worked for Cleveland as, for the second year in a row, Cribbs scored on a run, pass, and return.

Whether a kickoff, punt, or play from scrimmage, the Browns know they have a real "go-to guy."

JOSH GRIBBS

MAURICE JONES-DREW

RB, JACKSONVILLE JAGUARS
5-7, 208
UCLA

In blues music, the word "mojo" means spirit or power. A sad person is said to have "lost his mojo." The Jacksonville Jaguars never have that problem. They always have their own version of that energy and spirit, their own Mo-Jo: Maurice Jones-Drew. ("Mo" is often a nickname for Maurice.)

Though shorter than many running backs, Mo-Jo packs a powerful punch. He has scored at least 10 touchdowns in each of his four NFL seasons. He had his best season as a pro in 2009 when he set career highs with 1,391 rushing yards and 15 rushing TDs. He added 53 catches, including one for a touchdown. His powerful running made the Jaguars' offense go.

Mo-Jo has been patiently waiting for his time to shine. Until 2009, he was often paired with another back in Jacksonville, such as veteran Fred Taylor. As "the man" in 2009, he took advantage of his chance in a big way. He had a 61-yard TD run in Week 3 and then burst for an 80-yard score in Week 8.

Going long distance was nothing new for Jones-Drew. In his first two seasons, he was also the Jaguars' kickoff returner, and he took a pair of kicks to the house. As he settles into his full-time starting role, look for Mo-Jo to be rising!

CAREER STATS

Years	Att.	Rush Yds.	TDs	Rec.	Rec. Yds.	TD
4	842	3,924	49	201	1,782	5

MAURICE JONES-DREW

MARQUES COLSTON

WR, NEW ORLEANS SAINTS
6-4, 225
HOFSTRA UNIVERSITY

The 2009 season was one of "firsts and lasts" for Marques Colston. He will always be a member of the first Saints team to win a Super Bowl. And he'll be the last former Hofstra player to enjoy NFL success. Colston's tiny college doesn't have a football team anymore!

Saints fans are very glad that Hofstra had a team when Colston played, however. He joined the Saints as a seventh-round draft pick in 2006, but quickly became the team's number-one receiver. In fact, his 869 receiving yards in his first nine games is an all-time NFL best. In four NFL seasons, he has three 70-catch, 1,000-yard seasons (his only miss was in 2008, when he missed five games due to injury). In 2007, he set a Saints record with 98 catches. And he was Drew Brees' top target in 2009 with 70 catches and nine touchdowns as the Saints marched to their first NFL title. Colston added 15 catches and a touchdown in the postseason. In New Orleans' Super Bowl XLIV 31–17 win over Indianapolis, Colston tied for the team lead with seven catches and led the Saints with 83 receiving yards.

Colston's size and speed combine with a "go-for-the-gold" attitude to make him one of the NFL's most dangerous receivers. NFL defenders are probably glad that Hofstra has stopped making any more like him!

CAREER STATS			
Years	Rec.	Yards	TDs
4	285	4,074	33

MARQUES COLSTON

TONY GONZALEZ

TE, ATLANTA FALCONS
6-5, 243
UNIVERSITY OF CALIFORNIA

He's almost as big as a defensive lineman. He can dunk a basketball. He has hands like glue. And he's fast enough to put safeties on their heels. Is it Superman? No, it's just Tony Gonzalez, the superstar who has helped remake the tight end position. In 13 seasons with Kansas City and Atlanta, the former college hoops hero has been one of the NFL's top receiving threats and become one of the best all-time tight ends.

Gonzalez ended the 2009 season with 999 receptions, good for seventh-best all-time among *all* receivers, not just tight ends. In fact, he's the only TE in the top 20 in career catches. His 82 career touchdown catches are also a record for the position. He's topped 70 catches in a season 10 times, including a career-best and NFL-leading 102 in 2004.

Few athletes of Gonzalez's size have his delicate pass-catching skills and ankle-twisting moves. And fans enjoy his touchdown dunks over the crossbar, a skill picked up when he was a standout basketball player at Cal.

Along with San Diego's Antonio Gates and Dallas' Jason Witten, Gonzalez has turned the tight end into a valuable part of many NFL teams' offensive attacks. However, even with all those great tight ends out there, there's only one Tony Gonzalez.

CAREER STATS

Years	Rec.	Yards	TDs
13	999	11,807	82

TONY GONZALEZ

STEVE SMITH

WR, NEW YORK GIANTS
5-11, 195
UNIVERSITY OF SOUTHERN CALIFORNIA

For his first two NFL seasons, former college star Steve Smith of the Giants was "the other Steve Smith" in the NFL. Another player with that name was a star receiver for the Carolina Panthers. However, after a terrific 2009 season, fans now have two Pro Bowl Steve Smiths to watch. The Giants' young receiver had 107 catches for 1,220 yards and seven touchdowns. It was a breakthrough season—Smith of the Giants played in his first Pro Bowl—and will only add to fans' confusion in the years ahead!

CAREER STATS			
Years	Rec.	Yards	TDs
3	172	1,857	8

For the second year in a row, Smith was quarterback Eli Manning's favorite target, with almost twice as many catches in 2009 than any other Giants pass-catcher. However, his total of 107 was a big jump from a quiet 2008 season of only 57 catches. New York went with a more passing-heavy offense in 2009, and Smith was a big reason why.

In an era when many top receivers are tall (Terrell Owens, Randy Moss, Larry Fitzgerald), Smith uses his speed instead. He's only 5-11, not much bigger than many of the defenders he faces. So his key weapons are quickness, fleet feet, and perfect timing. And if he keeps putting up numbers like he did in 2009, he also won't need a name tag for fans to know who he is!

STEVE SMITH

JARED ALLEN
DE, MINNESOTA VIKINGS
6-6, 270
IDAHO STATE

Few players in the NFL seem to be having as much fun playing the game as Jared Allen. Of course, that's not the case for anyone who has to try and block this hard-charging defensive end.

Allen has become one of the NFL's best pass rushers in his six seasons, four with Kansas City and two with Minnesota. His go-for-broke style makes him hard to plan for. Though Allen is listed as a defensive end, the Vikings let him rush from just about anywhere on the line. Every opponent has to account for Allen on each play, or it's bad news for the quarterback.

If he could, Allen would probably play wearing a cowboy hat instead of a helmet. After he makes a sack, look for his mini-celebration. Calling on his Western heritage and rodeo experience from his youth in Montana, he pretends he's roping a calf instead of a quarterback. He's using up a lot of rope, too. Allen has had at least 10 sacks in four seasons, including a league-leading 15.5 in 2007 while he was with the Chiefs.

CAREER STATS		
Years	Sacks	Tackles
6	72	281

Allen's arrival in Minnesota in 2008 helped propel the Vikings to a pair of NFC North titles and a spot in the 2009 NFC Championship Game. As Allen looks to take the Vikings one more step to the Super Bowl, rest assured that he'll be having fun doing it! Opposing quarterbacks, of course, will not!

JARED ALLEN

DWIGHT FREENEY

DE, INDIANAPOLIS COLTS
6-1, 268
SYRACUSE UNIVERSITY

Dwight Freeney got off to a tremendous start in his NFL career . . . and he's hardly stopped in the eight seasons since. Drafted by the Colts after a great Syracuse career, Freeney forced nine fumbles as a rookie and recorded 13 sacks. He was an easy pick for the NFL Defensive Rookie of the Year, and came in second in voting for overall defensive player of the year. How could he top that? No problem; in his third season, he led the NFL in sacks with 16.

CAREER STATS		
Years	Sacks	Tackles
8	84	242

But there were still mountains to climb, so in 2006, Freeney's pass-rushing skills were crucial as the Colts reached the Super Bowl for the first time since the 1970 season. In that win over the Bears, Freeney recorded a key fumble recovery.

In 2009, Freeney just kept rolling over blockers and quarterbacks. On the way to Super Bowl XLIV, Freeney helped get the team off to a fast start. He had at least one sack in each of the team's first eight games, tying an NFL record. In that Super Bowl, Freeney battled back from an ankle injury to record the game's only sack.

Freeney has been destined for greatness since his rookie year, and he has come through again and again. On a team boasting several Hall of Fame defensive stars in its past, this five-time Pro Bowl selection is atop the Colts' all-time sack list. In 2010, he was named to the NFL's All-Decade Team for the 2000s. If he keeps this up, Freeney's next stop will be Canton, Ohio, and the Pro Football Hall of Fame.

DWIGHT FREENEY

ELVIS DUMERVIL

OLB, DENVER BRONCOS
5-11, 248
LOUISVILLE

First, the good news for NFL offensive lines: The Broncos' star linebacker Elvis Dumervil says he is only "eighty percent" comfortable at his position. The bad news, of course, is that 80 percent of Elvis is better than almost 100 percent of anyone else. If he can settle in even more comfortably . . . watch out!

Dumervil moved to linebacker only when the Broncos switched to a new defense in 2009. He was a defensive end before that. He had 8.5 sacks at that position as a rookie and jumped to 12.5 in his second season. That year, he also added an interception and recovered three fumbles.

Dumervil was a good defensive end, but Denver thought that his speed and size would make him a perfect NFL LB. They were right. In 2009, he got off to a super-hot start, notching 10 sacks in the team's first six games. Even after teams began double-teaming and game-planning around him, he added seven more to become the NFL leader with 17 by season's end. His quarterback-attacking skills earned Dumervil his first Pro Bowl selection.

And remember, that's only 80 percent!

Showing that he's a champ off the field as well, Dumervil was very involved with efforts to help Haiti after the January 2010 earthquake. He has more than 40 family members in that country and was one of the first NFL players to rally to that country's aid.

He'll continue to give 100 percent in that fight as he continues to improve his NFL game . . . and make life miserable for NFL blockers and QBs.

CAREER STATS

Years	Sacks	Tackles
4	43	129

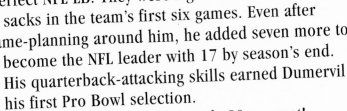

ELVIS DUMERVIL

PATRICK WILLIS

LB, SAN FRANCISCO 49ERS
6-1, 240
UNIVERSITY OF MISSISSIPPI

If a defender's main job is to tackle anyone carrying a football, then Patrick Willis is one of the best players in the NFL. He has been in the league for three years and twice has led in total tackles (174 in 2007 and 152 in 2009). Oh, yes, and he was also second overall in 2008 with 141 tackles!

Willis broke into the NFL with a splash, or should we say a *smash*? He was the 2007 NFL Defensive Rookie of the Year after leading the league in tackles.

CAREER STATS		
Years	Sacks	Tackles
3	9	467

He got even better, if you can imagine, in 2009. Along with another tackles title, he tied his career best with four sacks and set new career highs with three interceptions and three forced fumbles.

While 49ers fans certainly appreciate Willis, fantasy players hold him in special regard. In some leagues, players get points for tackles. That makes

him as valuable to some fantasy owners as a Peyton Manning or a Chris Johnson.

What separates Willis from other LBs is his speed and ability to read an offense. That means he can not only see the plays as they develop, but that he has the speed to get to where he needs to be very quickly. It's a rare combination and one that figures to keep him on top for a long time.

PATRICK WILLIS

DARRELLE REVIS

CB, NEW YORK JETS
5-11, 198
UNIVERSITY OF PITTSBURGH

The term "shutdown corner" perfectly describes Darrelle Revis. He is so good at covering opposing receivers that whole games might go by without the ball being thrown toward his side of the field.

Revis' excellent cover skills were a big part of the Jets' number-one defense in 2009. He was always matched against the top pass-catcher on the opponent . . . and he always took that player out of the game. Check out these big names that he held in check (with their 2009 single-game yardage totals vs. Revis): Andre Johnson (35), Randy Moss (24, 34), Terrell Owens (13), Steve Smith (5), Reggie Wayne (33). Those are Pro Bowl-caliber players, and Revis almost completely kept them out of the games.

And when teams do throw his way, he's just as likely to come back with the football. He had five interceptions in 2008 and another six in 2009, returning one each season for a score.

CAREER STATS

Years	Tackles	Int.
3	199	14

What makes Revis so good? It's a combination of speed and technique. He has the skills to stick with receivers of any size, but also the speed to keep up with the quicker ones. His study of their moves and the QB's looks also has given him a peek into what to expect. Put it all together, and you've got a player who finished second in the NFL Defensive Player of the Year voting . . . but who his coach calls the best cover corner he's seen since the amazing Deion Sanders almost 20 years ago.

DARRELLE REVIS

2009 NFL STANDINGS

AFC EAST
New England	10–6
N.Y. Jets	9–7
Miami	7–9
Buffalo Bills	6–10

AFC NORTH
Cincinnati	10–6
Baltimore	9–7
Pittsburgh	9–7
Cleveland	5–11

AFC SOUTH
Indianapolis	14–2
Houston	9–7
Tennessee	8–8
Jacksonville	7–9

AFC WEST
San Diego	13–3
Denver	8–8
Oakland	5–11
Kansas City	4–12

NFC EAST
Dallas	11–5
Philadelphia	11–5
N.Y. Giants	8–8
Washington	4–12

NFC NORTH
Minnesota	12–4
Green Bay	11–5
Chicago	7–9
Detroit	2–14

NFC SOUTH
New Orleans	13–3
Atlanta	9–7
Carolina	8–8
Tampa Bay	3–13

NFC WEST
Arizona	10–6
San Francisco	8–8
Seattle	5–11
St. Louis Rams	1–15

PLAYOFFS

Wild-Card Round

AFC

N.Y. Jets 24, Cincinnati 14
Baltimore 33, New England 14

NFC

Dallas 34, Philadelphia 14
Arizona 51, Green Bay 45

Divisional Round

AFC

Indianapolis 20, Baltimore 3
N.Y. Jets 17, San Diego 14

NFC

New Orleans 45, Arizona 14
Minnesota 34, Dallas 3

Championship Round

AFC

Indianapolis 30, N.Y. Jets 17

NFC

New Orleans 31, Minnesota 28 (OT)

SUPER BOWL XLIV
New Orleans 31, Indianapolis 17